**SELECTIONS FROM**

**100 GREATEST SONGS** of ROCK & ROLL

**1** VH Music First

HORN

T0055799

## Available for
**FLUTE, CLARINET, ALTO SAX, TENOR SAX, TRUMPET, HORN, TROMBONE, VIOLIN, VIOLA, CELLO**

Note: The keys in this book do not match the other wind instruments.

The following songs have been omitted from this publication because of licensing restrictions:
Johnny B. Goode
Jumpin' Jack Flash
Kashmir
Rock and Roll
Sympathy for the Devil
Whole Lotta Shakin' Goin' On

ISBN 978-1-4803-4136-4

**HAL•LEONARD® CORPORATION**
7777 W. BLUEMOUND RD. P.O. BOX 13819 MILWAUKEE, WI 53213

Visit Hal Leonard Online at
**www.halleonard.com**

# ALL ALONG THE WATCHTOWER

HORN

Words and Music by
BOB DYLAN

**Moderate Rock**

# ALL SHOOK UP

Horn

Words and Music by OTIS BLACKWELL
and ELVIS PRESLEY

# AMERICAN PIE

Horn

Words and Music by
DON McLEAN

D.S. al Coda

CODA

# BEAT IT

HORN

Words and Music by
MICHAEL JACKSON

# BLOWIN' IN THE WIND

Horn

Words and Music by
BOB DYLAN

# BLUE SUEDE SHOES

HORN

Words and Music by
CARL LEE PERKINS

# BORN TO BE WILD

Horn

Words and Music by
MARS BONFIRE

# BOHEMIAN RHAPSODY

HORN

Words and Music by
FREDDIE MERCURY

# BORN TO RUN

HORN

Words and Music by
BRUCE SPRINGSTEEN

**D.S. al Coda**

**CODA**

**Play 3 times**

# BRIDGE OVER TROUBLED WATER

HORN

Words and Music by
PAUL SIMON

# BROWN EYED GIRL

Horn

Words and Music by
VAN MORRISON

# BROWN SUGAR

HORN

Words and Music by MICK JAGGER
and KEITH RICHARDS

# CALIFORNIA DREAMIN'

Horn

Words and Music by JOHN PHILLIPS
and MICHELLE PHILLIPS

# CALIFORNIA GIRLS

Words and Music by BRIAN WILSON
and MIKE LOVE

Horn

# CRAZY

Horn

Words and Music by
WILLIE NELSON

# A DAY IN THE LIFE

HORN

Words and Music by JOHN LENNON
and PAUL McCARTNEY

**Tempo I**

# DREAM ON

HORN

Words and Music by
STEVEN TYLER

# EVERY BREATH YOU TAKE

Horn

Music and Lyrics by
STING

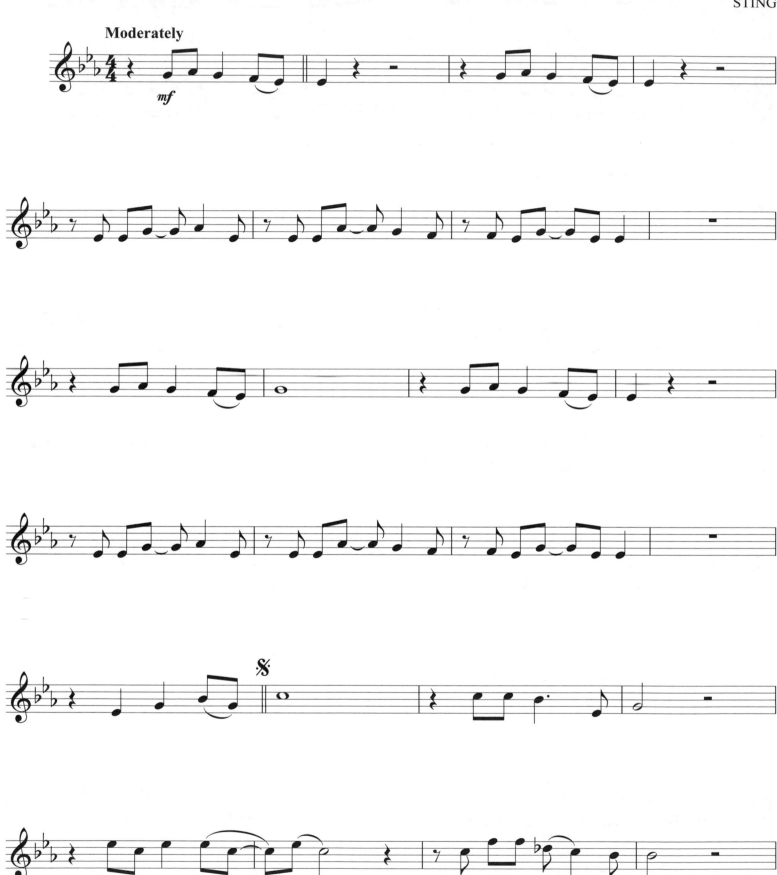

# FIRE AND RAIN

HORN

Words and Music by
JAMES TAYLOR

Fine

D.S. al Fine

# FOR WHAT IT'S WORTH

Horn

Words and Music by
STEPHEN STILLS

# FREE BIRD

Horn

Words and Music by ALLEN COLLINS
and RONNIE VAN ZANT

# GIMME SOME LOVIN'

Horn

Words and Music by STEVE WINWOOD,
MUFF WINWOOD and SPENCER DAVIS

# GLORIA

HORN

Words and Music by
VAN MORRISON

# GOD ONLY KNOWS

Horn

Words and Music by BRIAN WILSON
and TONY ASHER

# GOOD GOLLY MISS MOLLY

Horn

Words and Music by ROBERT BLACKWELL
and JOHN MARASCALCO

# GOOD VIBRATIONS

Horn

Words and Music by BRIAN WILSON
and MIKE LOVE

# GREAT BALLS OF FIRE

Horn

Words and Music by JACK HAMMER
and OTIS BLACKWELL

# A HARD DAY'S NIGHT

HORN

Words and Music by JOHN LENNON
and PAUL McCARTNEY

# HEARTBREAK HOTEL

Horn

Words and Music by MAE BOREN AXTON,
TOMMY DURDEN and ELVIS PRESLEY

# HEY JUDE

Horn

Words and Music by JOHN LENNON
and PAUL McCARTNEY

# HOTEL CALIFORNIA

Horn

Words and Music by DON HENLEY,
GLENN FREY and DON FELDER

# HOUND DOG

Horn

Words and Music by JERRY LEIBER
and MIKE STOLLER

# (I Can't Get No)
# SATISFACTION

HORN

Words and Music by MICK JAGGER
and KEITH RICHARDS

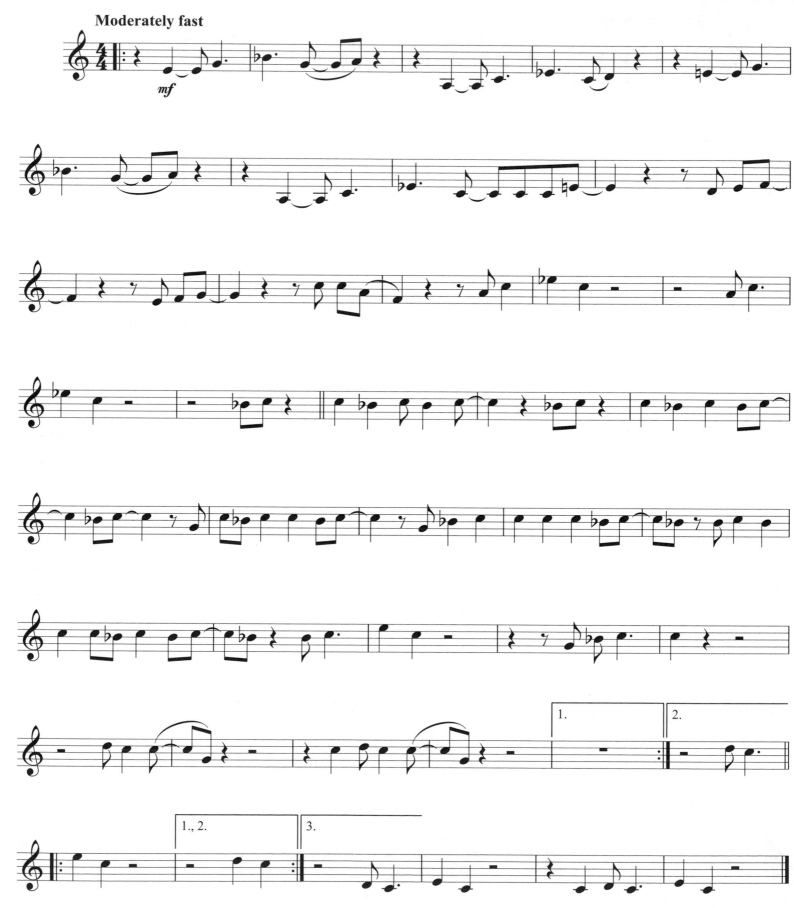

# I GOT YOU
## (I Feel Good)

Horn

Words and Music by
JAMES BROWN

# I HEARD IT THROUGH THE GRAPEVINE

Horn

Words and Music by NORMAN J. WHITFIELD
and BARRETT STRONG

# I WANT TO HOLD YOUR HAND

Horn

Words and Music by JOHN LENNON
and PAUL McCARTNEY

# IMAGINE

HORN

Words and Music by
JOHN LENNON

# IN THE MIDNIGHT HOUR

Horn

Words and Music by STEVE CROPPER
and WILSON PICKETT

# JAILHOUSE ROCK

Horn

Words and Music by JERRY LEIBER
and MIKE STOLLER

# JUMP

Horn

Words and Music by EDWARD VAN HALEN,
ALEX VAN HALEN and DAVID LEE ROTH

# LA BAMBA

HORN

By RITCHIE VALENS

**Moderate Latin Rock**

# LAYLA

HORN

Words and Music by ERIC CLAPTON
and JIM GORDON

# LET IT BE

HORN

Words and Music by JOHN LENNON
and PAUL McCARTNEY

Moderately slow

# LET'S STAY TOGETHER

Horn

Words and Music by AL GREEN,
WILLIE MITCHELL and AL JACKSON, JR.

# LIGHT MY FIRE

HORN

Words and Music by
THE DOORS

# LIKE A ROLLING STONE

Horn

Words and Music by
BOB DYLAN

# LONDON CALLING

Horn

Words and Music by JOE STRUMMER,
MICK JONES, PAUL SIMONON
and TOPPER HEADON

# LOUIE, LOUIE

HORN

Words and Music by
RICHARD BERRY

# MAGGIE MAY

Horn

Words and Music by ROD STEWART
and MARTIN QUITTENTON

# MORE THAN A FEELING

Horn

Words and Music by
TOM SCHOLZ

# MY GENERATION

Horn

Words and Music by
PETER TOWNSHEND

# MY GIRL

Horn

Words and Music by WILLIAM "SMOKEY" ROBINSON
and RONALD WHITE

# NO WOMAN NO CRY

Horn

Words and Music by
VINCENT FORD

# PAPA WAS A ROLLING STONE

Horn

Words and Music by NORMAN WHITFIELD
and BARRETT STRONG

# OH, PRETTY WOMAN

Horn

Words and Music by ROY ORBISON
and BILL DEES

# PIANO MAN

Horn

Words and Music by
BILLY JOEL

**Moderately slow, in 1**

# PROUD MARY

HORN

Words and Music by
JOHN FOGERTY

**Moderately**

# PURPLE HAZE

Horn

Words and Music by
JIMI HENDRIX

# RESPECT

Horn

Words and Music by
OTIS REDDING

# ROCK AROUND THE CLOCK

**Horn**

Words and Music by MAX C. FREEDMAN
and JIMMY DeKNIGHT

# ROXANNE

HORN

Music and Lyrics by
STING

# SEXUAL HEALING

Horn

Words and Music by MARVIN GAYE,
ODELL BROWN and DAVID RITZ

# SHE LOVES YOU

Horn

Words and Music by JOHN LENNON
and PAUL McCARTNEY

# (SITTIN' ON) THE DOCK OF THE BAY

Horn

Words and Music by STEVE CROPPER
and OTIS REDDING

# SMELLS LIKE TEEN SPIRIT

Horn

Words and Music by KURT COBAIN,
KRIST NOVOSELIC and DAVE GROHL

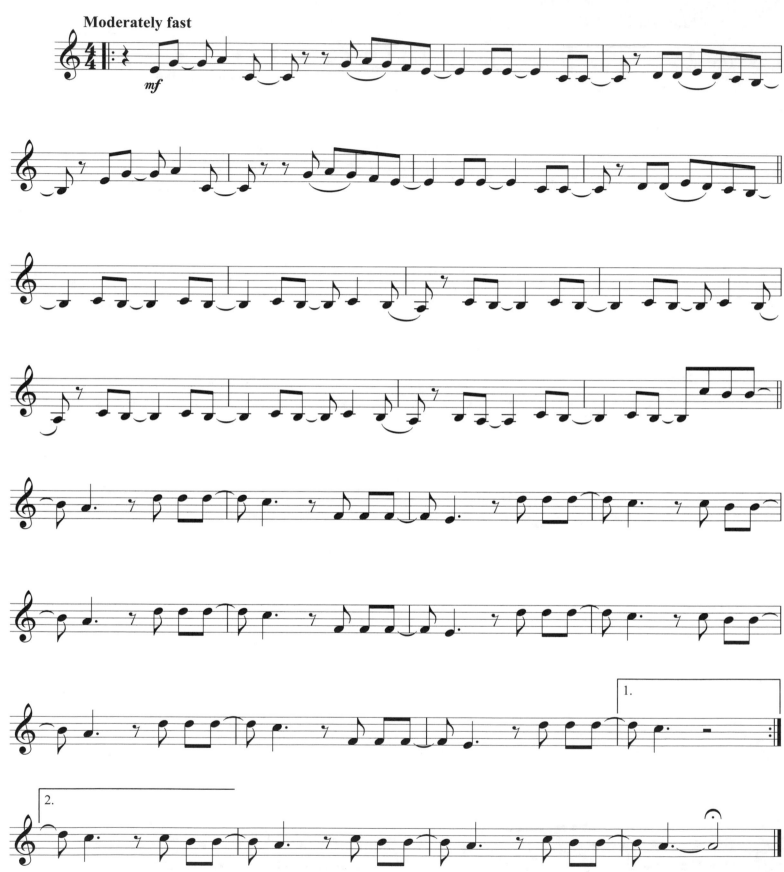

# SOMEBODY TO LOVE

Horn

Words and Music by
DARBY SLICK

# SPACE ODDITY

Horn

Words and Music by
DAVID BOWIE

Moderately slow

# STAIRWAY TO HEAVEN

Horn

Words and Music by JIMMY PAGE
and ROBERT PLANT

# STAND BY ME

Horn

Words and Music by JERRY LEIBER,
MIKE STOLLER and BEN E. KING

# START ME UP

Horn

Words and Music by MICK JAGGER
and KEITH RICHARDS

# STRAWBERRY FIELDS FOREVER

Horn

Words and Music by JOHN LENNON
and PAUL McCARTNEY

# STAYIN' ALIVE

HORN

Words and Music by BARRY GIBB,
ROBIN GIBB and MAURICE GIBB

# SUITE: JUDY BLUE EYES

HORN

Words and Music by
STEPHEN STILLS

# SUMMERTIME BLUES

Horn

Words and Music by EDDIE COCHRAN
and JERRY CAPEHART

# SUNSHINE OF YOUR LOVE

Horn

Words and Music by ERIC CLAPTON,
JACK BRUCE and PETE BROWN

**Moderate Rock**

# SUPERSTITION

Horn

Words and Music by
STEVIE WONDER

# TANGLED UP IN BLUE

HORN

Words and Music by
BOB DYLAN

# THAT'LL BE THE DAY

Horn

Words and Music by JERRY ALLISON,
NORMAN PETTY and BUDDY HOLLY

# THUNDER ROAD

HORN

Words and Music by
BRUCE SPRINGSTEEN

# THE TWIST

Horn

Words and Music by
HANK BALLARD

# TWIST AND SHOUT

Horn

Words and Music by BERT RUSSELL
and PHIL MEDLEY

# WALK THIS WAY

Horn

Words and Music by STEVEN TYLER
and JOE PERRY

# WE ARE THE CHAMPIONS

Horn

Words and Music by
FREDDIE MERCURY

# WE'VE ONLY JUST BEGUN

Horn

Words and Music by ROGER NICHOLS
and PAUL WILLIAMS

# WHAT'D I SAY

Horn

Words and Music by
RAY CHARLES

# WHAT'S GOING ON

Horn

Words and Music by RENALDO BENSON,
ALFRED CLEVELAND and MARVIN GAYE

# WHEN DOVES CRY

Horn

Words and Music by
PRINCE

# WHOLE LOTTA LOVE

Horn

Words and Music by JIMMY PAGE,
ROBERT PLANT, JOHN PAUL JONES,
JOHN BONHAM and WILLIE DIXON

# WILD THING

HORN

Words and Music by
CHIP TAYLOR

# WON'T GET FOOLED AGAIN

Horn

Words and Music by
PETER TOWNSHEND

**Moderately fast**

# YESTERDAY

Horn

Words and Music by JOHN LENNON
and PAUL McCARTNEY

Moderately

# YOU REALLY GOT ME

Horn

Words and Music by
RAY DAVIES

# YOU SHOOK ME ALL NIGHT LONG

Horn

Words and Music by ANGUS YOUNG,
MALCOLM YOUNG and BRIAN JOHNSON

Moderately fast

# YOUR SONG

Horn

Words and Music by
ELTON JOHN and BERNIE TAUPIN